Model Examines
A Graphic Poem

M. Anne Sweet

studioSixEight

$14.95

Model Examines

A Studio SixEight Book

ISBN-13: 978-0615556239 (Studio SixEight)
ISBN-10: 061555623X

STUDIO SIXEIGHT
Des Moines, WA

For Britny, Tina, Jo,
Carey, Stephani and others

Model Examines

From behind your camera
you tell me
you are brown not black—

I am
striped
blue
yellow
green—

You turn
my head
stretch
my
neck
dissolves
into
breast

I am
soft
and
pink—

i am brass-

I am Mona Lisa
in a
black dress
with
painted
toenails—

I am
a
black
and
purple
sun

a snake haloes my head—

I am shaman—
I am slave—

You do not ask
but I open
dressed and undressed—

Scored by
ship's
manifest—

a slave
in a
cargo
hold—

pink and brass breasts
flaming hair

the solstice   burning
                      inside
                      me—

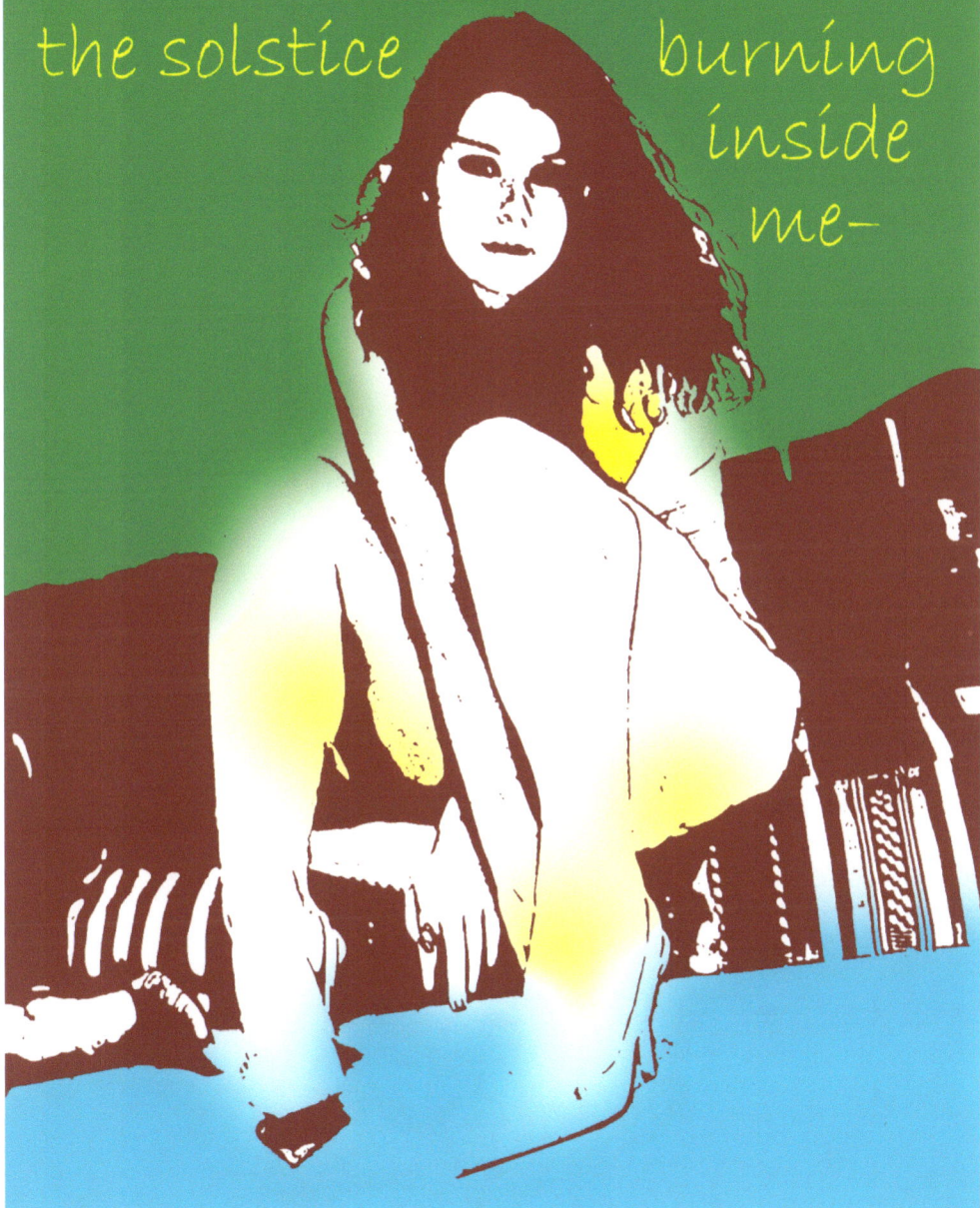

Model Examines
A Graphic Poem

The Original

The full-size original of "Model Examines" consists of 15 individual panels,

which were produced as giclées on canvas using archival inks.

Each panel is 14 inches wide by 20 inches high.

The entire installation is 70 inches wide by 60 inches high.

www.ingramcontent.com/pod-product-compliance
Lightning Source LLC
LaVergne TN
LVHW010026070426
835509LV00001B/25